A Voice for Stan

Kay Padley & Sue Pacey

Michael Terence
Publishing

First published in paperback by
Michael Terence Publishing in 2018
www.mtp.agency

ISBN 9781912639236

A Voice for Stan

Kay Padley & Sue Pacey

Introduction

This is a story of courage.

It is a type of courage I hope you never have to find within yourselves. It is outside most peoples' comprehension and is the stuff of nightmares.

It is also about devotion, selfless caring – and above all, love.

Even before we are born, the world in which we are nurtured is far from silent.

Early in his development a growing infant is capable of hearing and reacting to sound, even though those sounds are muffled by the protective amniotic fluid surrounding him.

He is soothed by the gentle thrum of his mother's heartbeat, her breathing, digestive process – and her voice. When he is born, that voice is already familiar as is her smell. It is not a coincidence that baby is laid on his mother's bare chest after birth, so he can reacquaint with those sounds and smells.

He becomes quiet with this skin-to-skin contact as she gently talks to him, actively turning his head to seek out her face. Even deaf babies do this as it is the vibrations they are sensitive to. Comforted, he seeks out the breast as without words he says, 'I'm here. Feed me, protect and nurture me.

Body language without need for words.

As he grows, he learns to communicate quickly by listening to those around him. He finds his voice and knows how to get attention by increasing the intensity of his cries until someone takes notice.

He learns to talk by copying, mimicking those close to him and, as he grows, those few words develop into sentences, all the way to reasoned conversation that allows him to engage with the world around him.

This happens so rapidly, we hardly notice it. We can all speak – can't we?

We all have a voice – haven't we?

So, what if that voice were suddenly taken away, leaving a one-way system of communication? Imagine going to sleep and when you wake you are unable to speak. Imagine not being able to make your wishes known or even to cry out for help when in difficulties. Then imagine never hearing your own voice again or being able to tell those closest how much you love them.

'I love you.'

The most evocative phrase in our vocabulary, said at your happiest and most tender moments – and one that you know you'll never be able to whisper again.

All of it happened to Kay and Stan.

This is their story.

Stan and Kay

How It All Began

How can I miss you when we've never met?

I wake each morning with your voice in my head

I look at my pillow and imagine you there

The feel of your skin and the smell of your hair

I love the messages you send me each day

They tease and feed my every thought

Although you are so far away

I feel you creeping into my heart

How can I miss you when we've never met?

Please tell me, my darling, so I won't forget

The feelings I have for you right here and now

Did I dream you into my life?

Please tell me how.

I could hardly believe my luck. Either that or the fates had decreed that 2003 was going to be my year. Life was going to improve. After two failed marriages and being alone for a while, it was time for *me* now.

My son, Matt was growing up and his dependence on me was getting less and less. At nineteen, he certainly felt he was completely mature – as we all do at that age. Throughout all the trials and tribulations, there had just been him and me. When he was younger, I'd had good reason to stay in – but now...?

Time for me, I thought, to reacquaint myself with another life that was no doubt still out there and one that involved adult company.

I'd had a few blind dates. That was an experience for anyone who'd not done it before. Some were no doubt nice, but others? Well, you quickly find out why they're on their own. Enough said!

But on this pleasant June evening, here I was off on another. I spent ages trying to decide which top to wear with my spotted black and white skirt. It made me look thinner – we girls *always* like to look thinner. I say 'girls.' I was 43 and felt it was about time I found a soulmate and settled down.

So, after another forage through the wardrobe, I finally decided on a black top, wanting to look my best. Unlike other liaisons before, we'd been e-mailing and chatting to each other for about three months – and it felt good. The time had come to meet.

I loved the sound of his voice with its soft Liverpudlian accent – a deep, soothing tone that I'd cheerfully have listened to all day. During that three months, I'd already learned quite a lot about him.

Stan was such an intelligent man. That was obvious just by talking to him, not just what he said but the way he said it. He seemed to know the most obscure things. Just the type of chap you wanted on your team at a pub quiz! And always that accent – that magical accent. I knew that if I allowed it to, that voice would lull me to sleep one day.

And here I was taking that first step on the ladder to yet another part of my life. Was I nervous as I locked up my car and went to meet him? You bet I was!

Quickly, I straightened my skirt and looked around for a black Saab – and there it was parked a short distance away. He got out, smiling broadly. He was wearing a smart, dark suit and I remember wondering what he was doing with a jacket on when it was so warm. But, I liked what I saw as we walked into the pub together.

'I can't stop long.' I heard myself say. 'I've got a new kitten and I've got to get back to her.' Why I said it, I don't know. It must have sounded like an excuse.

When I meet someone, the first thing I notice is their eyes, then their hands. As he collected our drinks and sat down, I found myself looking into a pair of lovely blue eyes that were soft and gentle. But he kept looking down as if nervous. Either that, or he didn't like the look of me. An alarm bell rang somewhere in my subconscious.

Then, he seemed to relax and began to talk. That's when I noticed his hands. Strong hands with long, slender fingers and well-manicured nails. The alarm bell became silent.

He'd come straight from work – hence the suit. He worked in Windsor in IT. Although my geography was rubbish, I guessed that must have been quite a journey, though he said he travelled around quite a lot. I began to warm to this rather serious man who I bet was new to the dating game. He'd worked in both Saudi Arabia and Egypt for some time – around seven years. I was pleased to see he didn't drink and drive and happy to sit there talking with a Coke in front of him. I never drink when I'm driving, preferring orange juice.

I was becoming relaxed in his company. No matter how many times you've spoken on-line or by phone, meeting is a whole new ball game and neither of us had the confidence that comes with that first flush of youth. But, he seemed a bit distant and not really interested in me.

We nearly didn't meet at all. Just before we first got in touch, Stan was thinking of moving to France. All the e-mails and phone calls had seemed to make him change his mind.

Our first meeting was over too quickly, but nevertheless, I decided to take the initiative and ask if he wanted to see me again. I stood silently in the car park looking at him and dreading the answer.

'Most definitely,' he said without hesitation, but said he'd wondered if the remark about having to get back was because *I* didn't like the look of *him*. Nothing could have been further from the truth. I told him so with a nervous laugh.

'Then why don't we sit in my car and talk privately?' he said. I got in and we talked – properly this time – more relaxed in each other's company. By the time we parted, I knew one thing. I was in love with his mind and his voice. Perhaps the rest would come later.

We arranged to meet at his place in a fortnight's time as the following week he was meeting a few friends from a band he used to be in for a 'jam' session in Liverpool. He played guitar and said he was having lessons on the double bass, which explained the huge case on the back seat.

I thought over our meeting long and hard over the coming days and how I'd nearly blown it over the adorable black kitten I'd got from the animal shelter a few weeks before, in my nervousness to say at least something sensible.

Stan and I were not alike. We moved in different worlds. He'd never been married. I had. Stan lived alone. I had Matt, though he did seem to treat the place like a hotel, often staying out with various mates or at his girlfriend's. He was reasonably good at letting me know where he was, with the odd, 'I'm not a baby, Mum.' But he was – my only baby and perhaps it would only be when he'd children of his own that he'd realise just how special that relationship is. No matter how old they are.

'So now,' I told the soft, ball of fluff, 'no more shinning up my legs with your claws out, Madam, and scratching my fake tan. I want to look good from now on.' I had a reason to for the first time in ages.

It's probably a very old and overused cliché, but it was love at first sight for both of us. Here we were, both in our 40's, feeling like a couple of teenagers in the first throes of passion. It took us a while to confess it, but after that second meeting it was obvious we were meant to be together. We have one life, so why spend it apart?

The need to be together was such that Stan moved into my house in July. He still worked away during the week and I'd write him poetry to read while he was away. It filled the evenings when he was not at home and I could sit, write and count my blessings.

If my world should end tomorrow, I really wouldn't care

The love we shared these past few weeks was so precious and so rare

You've made me feel alive again to face each and every day

Thoughts of you have touched my heart in a very special way.

I love to hear your 'scouser's' voice. It makes me tingle and glow

I love you so incredibly – much more than I think you know.

And if your face was the very last thing that I was meant to see

It would give me so much joy to know that you were loved by me.

*****

Later that month, he proposed, and I didn't *actually* turn him down, but…

It was a huge step and I talked him into living

together for a bit longer. I'd lost my mum recently and knew she wouldn't be there. And I wanted to lose some weight. I'd put it on courtesy of an underactive thyroid gland. Stan saw through it all and stated firmly that he'd marry me even if I was wearing a black bag and we had to drag two people off the street to be witnesses.

With the proceeds from both our houses, we bought a bungalow together. It would be ours – somewhere we could spend the rest of our lives together. I gave up work. Stan's job was enough to support the two of us. We were happy and content.

2004 ended and a new year began. We were having a meal and afterwards, Stan suddenly got down one knee and proposed again. This time I had no qualms and accepted ... but only if *he* changed his name to mine. I'd reverted to my maiden-name.

'What's in a name?' he said and readily agreed.

Stan and Kay on their wedding day

We decided not to wait any longer and get on with it and were married at Sheffield Register Office on the 18th February and after a reception at the Norton Hotel, left for a blissfully happy honeymoon in Malta. We had a fantastic suite with twin balconies overlooking the ocean and the sun shone throughout. Ten wonderful days of happiness! It all felt perfect.

Life was wonderful and one of the greatest things was eating together.

We loved to go out for meals and did it as often as we could. Stan's favourite was steak and kidney pie and chips. But if we wanted a treat, he'd book a really nice restaurant and it would be steak. He liked his rare, unlike me. I prefer my food dead.

When we met, Stan was over sixteen stone – cuddly – it was clear he got a great deal of pleasure from eating. He loved puddings. His favourite was yummy chocolate cake with lashings of cream or ice cream.

Sitting together eating and talking is one of life's pleasures. We could relax, take our time and mull over the day's events. It didn't matter whether we were out somewhere posh, dressed to the nines or at home wearing slippers, at the kitchen table. We could take our time and enjoy being together.

That's the problem with being on your own, you so rarely sit and eat with anyone else. We'd both had quite enough of that in the past.

We went out a lot, Scarborough, York, Chester and Whitby which I wasn't keen on. It brought on my phobia of birds. I hate seagulls. The things would ambush you if they thought you'd got anything remotely edible. Stan used to laugh and say, 'Stick close to the buildings in the shadows, Kay. They won't get you there!' He walked on the outside of the pavement, not to protect me from sharp, pecking beaks, but because he was a gentleman. He opened doors for me, placing his hand gently in the middle of my back to let me go first. I suppose it's a bit old fashioned now that sort of thing, but I loved it. At last someone loved me enough to do those special little things that meant so much.

The subject of children came up almost as soon as we moved in together. I had Matt, but Stan didn't have any of his own. I know he'd have made a great dad, but I was 43 and the biological clock was ticking. A pregnancy would have been difficult due to previous blood clotting problems. I'd got a bad back and my health wasn't brilliant, so we talked about fostering or adopting. We agreed to wait until Stan got a job closer to home. Nevertheless, it didn't stop us having the plans drawn up for an extension. It was easy as we had the same tastes when it came to furniture and decoration. And, as well as an extra bedroom for a possible addition to our little family, we planned a bit of luxury for ourselves as well – a large en-suite and a jacuzzi with lights. The adjoining bedroom was to have a huge window in the ceiling, so we could lie in bed and look at the stars.

We had our dreams, soon to be reality and it seemed that all he wanted was to make me happy and I him. I think his natural kindness and equanimity came from looking after his mother in her last years. Although he'd two brothers, one in Canada, it had been expected that Stan, being free and single would do all the odd jobs, take her shopping after work and generally be there to see to her needs. And he did it willingly.

When I met her, she seemed to like me at first, but as soon as Stan stated his intention to move in with me, all that changed. She promptly took him out of her will and left everything to his other two brothers. It caused an enormous rift in the family which was never resolved even when she died.

Through it all though, we always believed that you must take every chance for happiness whenever it may present itself. We have one life and must live it. This is not a rehearsal!

And we found our happiness in our little corner of the world. Neither of us will ever regret taking that step, because we'd found each other and that's all we needed. It was regretful but not important what other people thought.

I loved his little ways; the way he looked at me; the way he did things and that lovely Liverpudlian voice. The sound of his voice still resounds, there in my head. Above all, he made me feel safe. 'I'll protect you from the Hooded Claw, Kay!' That was the main antagonist of Hanna-Barbera's Penelope Pitstop.

And now?

I miss all those little idiosyncrasies terribly. I mourn the loss of them. I crave them. It's the small things we all take for granted, never giving them a second thought until one day, they're ripped from your grasp.

That's what was to happen. And never in my darkest nightmares did I ever imagine that something so terrible would ever happen to us.

Stan's hip was giving him some discomfort. It was becoming difficult getting in and out of the car and walking for any distance – a peril of approaching middle age and the natural progression of wear and tear according to the doctor. He saw a specialist quickly. We were fortunate in having private medical insurance which had been a benefit of his job.

He was told that the whole situation could be improved by a small operation which involved scraping the inside of the joint. Neither of us were worried and he'd had a general anaesthetic before for a hernia repair, so it wasn't a big deal.

The surgeon said he could operate in three days' time. The irony was not lost on me that money may not talk, but it sure gets the wheels moving quickly. I was grateful that Stan hadn't a prolonged wait with constant pain. Some unfortunate people are waiting months.

The night before the operation, I lay in my husband's arms in our bed. Something was bothering me and keeping me awake. My stomach was churning. Maybe it was the sheer speed of how events had unfolded, and I hadn't organised it properly in my mind. On the other hand, I reasoned, surely it was good with not so much time to worry about it. And, he'd be off work for six weeks and we could be together every day.

'A simple operation' the surgeon had said. 'A bit of arthritis, that's all. We can resurface the joint. I've done this operation many times. It's not a hip replacement. At only 49, you're far too young for that.'

But, despite all his reassuring words, I was worrying, and I didn't know why.

I left Stan the night before his surgery in a single room in the private wing of the hospital.

Emmerdale had just started and as I kissed him, the last thing he said was 'I love you.'

'Love you too,' I replied. 'See you tomorrow, darling.'

I love you. The last words he would ever say to me.

*****

March 6th 2008

The date was to be burned indelibly into my memory.

After I left Stan in hospital, I'd managed to get some sleep, though it felt strange without him beside me. I remember looking at the clock when I woke, realising that it would soon be time to phone the hospital to speak to Stan before he went to the theatre. He had a phone in his room and we'd agreed to speak around 9am as his operation was scheduled for 10am.

On getting no reply from his room, I called Reception and was told that he'd been taken down early as the previous patient had cancelled. I was bitterly disappointed not to have spoken to him before he went.

'You'll just have to get on with the day then, Kay,' I told myself. At least it would all be over sooner.

I hadn't any orders to fill for my greeting card business, so concentrated on the stock, anxious to keep both body and mind active with routine things on this far-from-routine day. I loved my work and the creativity required to produce something beautiful. I concentrated on keepsakes and cards for special occasions and had regular buyers that came back time after time. Stan had always helped me when it came to the printing and my shop on E-Bay was doing well. I was proud of my100% feedback as all the designs were my own.

Later, I did a little housework to fill the time when Sister said Stan would be back from the recovery room. The next couple of hours passed with painful slowness, despite my looking at the clock every few minutes. I swear those hands never moved.

By twelve, I could wait no longer and picked up the phone.

As I dialled, my heart was pounding, my mouth dry. I remember it so well, telling myself not to be silly. I steadied the receiver with both hands. The nurse said that Stan wasn't back from the recovery room yet and could I ring again in a couple of hours?

Oh no, not another 2 hours to worry! I thought. *Do something, Kay.*

It was a lovely day for early March and not in the least cold. I decided to go to the Post Office to mail a parcel. My ever-reliable car started first time.

Standing in the usual queue at the counter, I told myself I'd better get used to making these trips as Stan wouldn't be driving for a few weeks at least.

From the other side of the counter, Lynn's voice broke my reverie. 'Heard anything yet, Kay?' She always took my parcels and we frequently chatted about our families.

'Not yet,' I said. 'Just heading home to call the hospital. It seems that Stan likes a good sleep after an anaesthetic.' I smiled, and she returned it. I jumped in the car and drove home quickly.

He still hadn't returned to the ward. Now, I was *really* worried, my heart thudding against my ribs. I paced the room, now convinced that something *was* wrong, then stared out of the window at the clear sky.

The phone rang loudly, and I jumped. Fumbling, I grabbed the receiver.

It was the anaesthetist, his voice steady and matter of fact. Had Stan ever had a problem coming out of anaesthetic in the past? I said he'd been very sleepy after his hernia operation but had been okay afterwards. 'Would you like to come now, Mrs Padley?' he asked. 'I'll see you when you get here.'

I grabbed my coat and bag and jumped in the car. Although only a ten-minute journey, it was end of school time and seemed to take forever.

I was taken to Stan's room and told that someone would be down very soon to talk to me. Would I like a cup of tea? There was no bed in the room, just an empty space where my husband should have been, awake but drowsy and telling me he was okay.

The anaesthetist arrived almost immediately and sat facing me. He explained that as Stan was coming out of the anaesthetic, he became very agitated and required sedation to settle him. When it didn't pass, he was taken for an MRI scan. It showed damage to three major areas of his brain.

It was like being hit with a hammer. No words would come. No emotion. Just stunned silence as the room began to close in around me.

'We'll take you to see your husband now, Mrs Padley.' It seemed like a disembodied voice from somewhere far away, my ability to think suspended by shock. I was unable to move. 'The nurse will come and take you to see your husband.'

Fumbling for my mobile, I phoned Matt, blubbering and almost incoherent by the time he answered.

'I'm sorry, Mum. I can't understand you,' he said gently.

'Just come ... to the hospital,' I managed to stammer.

'Okay, Mum. I'm on my way.'

A nurse came into the room and walked with me to the recovery area outside the theatres, where people are taken directly after surgery.

My Stan hadn't woken up. He lay on his back in the bed and just looked as though he was still asleep. I took his hand and kissed him on the cheek, not knowing what to think or say. I just wanted to touch him – for him to open his eyes, look at me and smile as though it had all been a horrible mistake. I wanted to hear his voice, his laughter and all the things that made him Stan.

'We're taking him to the Intensive Care Unit, where we can look after him better and he can get the best treatment, Kay.'

'Now, I was 'Kay.' Formality had been abandoned. Had hope gone with it? I didn't even want to think about that. Silently, I stood biting the inside of my lip as his bed was pushed away and I was taken to yet another waiting room.

Matt arrived, and he'd brought a friend of mine for support. He was angry. 'What have you done to Stan?' he demanded of the surgeon. 'What happened?'

It surprised me as the two of them had never really got on, but I think he saw my pain and hurt. He needed to ask the right questions – be the strong one and defend me – because I was too distressed to do so.

'You can go in now, Kay,' said the nurse gently. My friend had to stay outside the room and Matt said he would too, having a terrible phobia of needles.

I looked in desperation at the nurse. I was in a bubble, alone. It was just me then, and how alone I felt walking into that room where my husband lay surrounded by equipment, flashing lights and alien noises.

Stan had been connected to a ventilator that was breathing for him. There were tubes and drips everywhere. I sat on the chair provided and was almost afraid to take his hand for fear someone might make me let go. For while ever I was holding his hand… well, it wasn't real and nothing bad would happen. Tears flowed unimpeded down my cheeks.

I looked in disbelief at the nightmare that was unfolding around me, words hammering in my head. 'A simple procedure. Done it many, many times.' 'Bye… See you tomorrow, darling.' 'I love you, Kay.'

The surgeon pulled up a chair beside me and sat. 'We don't know what it is that actually happened, not yet, Kay.'

I wanted to see Stan's brain scan. God knows why! I needed to grab some shred of understanding. Anything to hang on to by my fingertips. I remember looking at it and the areas of damage being pointed out. Shadows – three of them and, it was only when I saw it did I started to believe that this was real. It was not some horrible mistake.

'He may not be the same man you knew. The way he thinks and handles life may change. His personality and moods may be altered. The fact is, we really don't know until he wakes up. We'll be able to tell you more then.' I stared into the doctor's face as he spoke.

Wake up, Stan. Please wake up and tell me you're okay.

I was having difficulty taking in his words. It was as though we were discussing a random person, not my husband. It resembled one of those films where someone's voice just fades into the background. Profound weakness overtook me as if all the air had been kicked violently from my body. There was no anger, just an almighty pain in the middle of my chest.

Anger would come later.

What have you done? A simple operation. It was only a simple operation, done many… many…

Matt took me home and I cried myself to sleep, alone in our bed, clutching Stan's t-shirt that he'd worn two nights previously when our world had been a very different place.

In the past few hours that world had been shattered.

When something so dreadful happens, it's not the magnitude of the event that is so difficult to cope with – not at first. You're in such a state of confusion and overwhelming shock, it acts as a bit of a buffer. You run on adrenaline and seize on to every bit of hope and positive news that you can. The flicker of an eyelid, an involuntary sigh or movement is what you crave until you wonder if you imagined them. If wishes were horses, beggars would ride. And I wished, begged, prayed and talked to anyone who would listen. And I hoped.

It's the hope that almost kills you and grief is the price we pay for love.

I sat by Stan's side all day, every day willing him to wake up, even though I knew he was being kept unconscious by strong drugs and the machine breathing for him. They said it was to allow his brain to repair itself and for any swelling to go down.

The Intensive Care Unit was a very alien place to me.

I'd never seen anything like that before. There were no curtains round the few specialised beds and endless banks of machinery, all blipping, flashing and bleeping. In a nearby bed was a young man, clearly restless and he kept waving his arms about. I couldn't understand why Stan wasn't doing that. There was an older man sitting with him and, at some point, we found ourselves together in the coffee room.

'Is that your son?' I asked.

He told me it was, and that the boy was an addict and had taken a huge overdose. I was consumed by anger. My Stan had done nothing and was fighting to live and here was this man's son in a self-inflicted predicament trying to end his, whether intentional or not.

Stan lay still in the bed on his back. My lovely big husband showed no signs of life other than the noises from the ventilator. I held his hand, massaging it gently and willing it to move.

Seven days later, Stan was moved to the High Dependency area and placed in a single room off the main corridor. Little had changed but at least we could have more privacy. At this point the medical staff began to reduce the sedation to allow him to wake up, but it seemed to have little effect.

A couple of friends who were in the Salvation Army visited and prayed for him to wake. They were full of faith and hope and clearly devout believers, whilst I felt nothing but despair. 'Don't pray for him to wake until he's ready.' I pleaded, fearing if he did then he'd be a cabbage. My Stan wouldn't have wanted to live life like that. It wasn't living.

I knew that if *that* were to be the case, *I'd* have to have done something about it. This was the man I was in love with, my soul-mate, my life. I couldn't bear the mere thought of his existence in a persistent vegetative state. And constantly, I was asking myself how could this be? For someone to be there in the morning, laughing, talking, telling me he loved me and a few hours later, all that gone. It was like a record playing forever in my head.

Then, one day as I sat there, Stan opened his eyes. I wept though it was clear he didn't know who I was. It was just an empty gaze. A few days later they removed the tracheostomy tube to see if he could breathe on his own. After a few heart-stopping moments, he did.

At times in the days that followed, Stan became very restless to the extent that a mattress was put on the floor in case he fell, despite the cot-sides. When I arrived, he would become calmer, staying where he was and not trying to climb out. He would lie still and stare at me. I would stroke his face and sing softly to him, but there was still not one spark of recognition in those empty eyes. 'It's okay, Stan.' I whispered. 'I'm here.'

'Thank goodness you are, Kay,' said the nurse. 'You're the only one who can calm him.'

As I looked into those steady, staring blue eyes, I knew that somehow a spark of the memory of my voice must have remained.

It was May, two months since the surgery. Stan had picked up C Difficile from somewhere, vulnerable in his weakened state to everything that was going. He'd been terribly ill and had lost a great deal of weight. Unable to speak or eat, as well as the intravenous fluids fed into his arm, a feeding tube had been inserted directly into his stomach. He was fed a liquid diet through it rich in vitamins and minerals.

Because of the infection, everything that entered his room had to be either bagged and disposed of or disinfected. I'd covered the walls of his room with laminated posters of his beloved Liverpool FC to try and provide some stimulation. On this particular day, Matt was visiting and had a laptop with pictures of the team on. He placed it in front of Stan.

'Point to Torres,' he said.

Stan stared at the screen.

'If you understand what I'm saying, Stan,' I said, 'point to Torres.'

Stan raised his arm towards the footballer. My hands shot up to my face at this huge breakthrough, though I could hardly believe it.

'Stan, if you understand me, close your eyes.'

His eyes left the screen and looked at me. For a few moments, he stared, then closed his eyes. I ran from the room to tell the nurse. It was the sign I needed to shake me from the torpor and hopelessness of the past weeks – my cue to get proactive and do something.

I made a set of flash cards with 'YES' on one side and 'NO' on the other. Stan looked bemused and I had to show him how to use them. It was as though he had to learn to think again and re-learn all the simple skills we take for granted. I had to show him how to turn them over. He was like a blank canvas on which everything had to be re-written.

I brought in a Scrabble set to see if he recognised the

simple words that went with the pictures. Sometimes he did, more often he didn't, and I tried to get him to draw a line to what was say, a cat or a dog, but he needed help to even hold the pencil. His right hand didn't work at all and of course, he was right-handed. It was a daunting task, but it kept me focussed. I knew deep down that if Stan was to progress, it was going to be down to me. He was my husband and I was going to fight for him – whatever that took.

I made up little games – God knows I'd plenty of time to think of things during the hours, days and weeks I spent in that room. One was about matching animals to the things that they liked e.g. birds like seed, dogs like a ball and cats like milk. I was astounded when he matched 'cat' to 'cheese' as our cat, Zoe has a particular liking for it. Somewhere buried deep in memory were things he clearly *did* remember. They just needed coaxing out, slowly, repeatedly and with patience. It needed love and I had plenty of that to give him, even if it took the rest of my life.

But the anger remained.

Weeks later, a speech therapist came breezing into the room and introduced herself. She'd come armed with flash cards and a Scrabble set! I was almost speechless at the lost time and opportunities had I not been there. I got the impression that he was considered too damaged and had been shoved in a room to get on with it. She told me how well I was doing and beat a hasty retreat. On that point, she was wise.

I began to think how I could strengthen the arm he could use, so I took in a tin of baked beans with a note taped to it that said, 'Stan's exercising tool.' The first time he tried to hold it above his head he all but knocked himself out, but we persevered till he got it with me guiding his hand.

He managed to stand with the help of two physiotherapists, one either side, but it seemed he'd forgotten how to walk – or that particular motor pathway in his brain had been damaged. All this time the infection had been a recurring problem and it was very slow to clear. Still incontinent, he would contaminate his hands and try to pull the pad off which added to the problem. The nurses were unable to always come straight away to change him and I discovered why he became so restless and tried to climb out of the bed. C Diffiicile burns the skin. He couldn't stand the pain of sitting in a mess. It is so important that with this condition the patient is changed straight away, or sores quickly appear. It must have been unbearable for him.

Progress was very slow – in all things. He got tired very easily but was beginning to understand me. I told him what had happened to him because I don't think he knew and he pointed to his scar. 'This is only temporary, Stan,' I said. 'We *are* going to get you better.' Tears rolled down his cheeks and it almost broke my heart.

Can you imagine waking up in an alien place and having no memory of how you got there or what had happened to you. You have drips in your arms. You can't move one of them and there's a boxing glove on the other. You don't know why you're imprisoned in this bed and you can't speak, make a sound or even cry out. I often question why he didn't go mad!

We'd reached the point where Stan needed intensive physiotherapy and I enquired about him being transferred to nearby Walton hospital. This houses the Stroke Unit, and, after all, Stan's symptoms were very similar. I was told that he wasn't suitable. I don't think they'd take him because of the recurrent infection. More frustration. It seemed as though I was the only one trying to push forward all the time. More anger. In desperation, I contacted our local MP and explained what had happened and what the current situation was and, as if by magic, a bed at Walton became available. I remain indebted to her. He was moved there in the August – a full five months after the operation.

The expected intense physiotherapy was not forthcoming and whatever was done, took place in the room. He wasn't allowed in the corridors due to the risk of infection. The nurses told me they didn't think he was in the right place, but when I asked where they thought he should have been, they didn't know. In the confines of his small single room, Stan became very restless and agitated. I was beside myself with frustration.

One more person to ask, one more person to tell

Why can't people just leave me alone? This is a living hell.

Alone with fear, anger and sadness no one could ever imagine

My whole world has fallen apart. Why did God allow such madness?

Once a strong, intelligent man, full of honour, passion and love

Now a shadow of his former self, I look up and ask God above.

Why have you allowed this to happen? Is it because I've been bad?

You didn't prepare me for this one. I think I might go mad.

Please send me someone to guide me and tell me what to do.

For I cannot function without him. It seems I only have you.

Give me the strength to carry the load for I know my son needs me.

I go through the every-day motions, but this pain isn't meant to be.

The agony of looking at Stan knowing he doesn't understand,

Breaks my heart into pieces. He was such a lovely man.

He used to say that his aim in life was to love and make me happy

And how he was so very proud to have me as his wife.

He asked a minimum of twenty years – and that I thought we had.

Oh, how can life be so very cruel to make us both so sad?

And now, he can't say anything...but his eyes say it all

Like a child in a man's body: and he doesn't know anyone at all.

*****

My husband needs to be at home. Not in this sterile environment where there's no future for him. He's never going to get better here... nor make progress. I can do what they're doing for him here and I can do it better. I can provide the stimulation he needs. I can do the physio. I can be there day and night. I want my husband home and I want it to happen now before anything more terrible happens to him – if that's conceivable.

And, I want it now!

A great deal had to be arranged and it took 3 months to organise. I was asked to do two twelve-hour shifts to assess my ability to cope, regardless of anything else that had been put in place. I was to stay at the hospital and they would find me a bed to sleep on beside Stan.

When it came to it however, there *was* no bed and the best they could do was a reclining chair. *'Great!'* I thought. Anyone who has tried to sleep on one of those things will know exactly what I mean especially with my bad back! I suffer from scoliosis in my upper back and have to sleep propped up to avoid the vertigo that comes along with it.

Stan was fed by a peg. This is a tube that goes through the abdominal wall directly into his stomach, by-passing the eating process we all take for granted. They showed me how to do his feeds using a syringe, as well as all the other care he was going to need. I must have passed the test!

Finally, we had a date for Stan to go home. It was the 15th October, so I made a wall chart and we crossed off the days. Then, something happened, in relation to his care package. Not everything was in place and it was all delayed another week. Stan became very petulant and difficult. Not particularly with me, but it was the nurses who bore the brunt of his aggression. Finally, a hospital bed was delivered to our home and all the care on a day-by-day basis planned down to the last detail.

No one still had any idea what had happened to Stan to have left him the way he was. There was no actual proof that any negligence had occurred and no one individual could be proven to be at fault. What everyone in a similar situation wants are reasons *why* something happens. Even though the reality of it all slowly sinks in, somehow having a reason brings a sort of conclusion. We didn't have that because no one *knew* what had happened. I'd been to see a Solicitor of course, who'd advised me that unless we could prove negligence there could be no compensation claim to help with Stan's care which he would need for the rest of his life. Had he not had his surgery privately, we could have sued the hospital. But not apparently if you pay!

I'd been advised by so many 'well-meaning' people to put him in a home and get on with my life. I wanted to hit out. This was my husband who I loved, and the man I'd planned to spend the rest of my life with. I was going to – just not in the way we'd dreamed of nor planned for.

The prospect of Stan coming home should have, at the very least, been daunting. It wasn't. All I could focus on was that if he was at home, I could work on him and concentrate on what he *could* do and not what he'd been robbed of. He was on loads of medication for pain and stuff to prevent fits, as was normal with any brain injury. One was a drug called Tegretol, and the side-effects were to depress and calm the brain, thinking and movement all becoming slowed down. It was hard to know what was due to the drugs, and what was because of the brain injury.

I remember vividly the day Stan came home. They carried my husband in on a stretcher and placed him on the bed in the newly-converted bedroom. He was so weak, he could hardly lift his head or indicate yes and no. But all I felt was joy at having him home – a day I thought would never come and so that was good enough for me. He was home – my Stan – he'd come back to me. I was grateful for small mercies.

I'd rigged up an electronic doorbell with an attachment he could squeeze to attract attention, because it was not realistic that I could be in the same room *all* the time. There were things I'd have to do and anyhow, I don't think Stan would have wanted that.

When talking to a friend, I'd stated my intention to convert a room into a games-room. At the time, it must have seemed a wacky idea I suppose. But, I knew how Stan thought. We were always so in tune. It seemed that I was the only one who was daring to look to the future – of the man he could be again – and not like all the rest who seemed to have written him off. They only saw what was here and now. A silent shell of a man lying in a bed, unable to eat, speak or walk.

But I dared and, with a small insurance pay-out had the room decorated in his beloved Liverpool colours. An artist painted the club's emblem on one wall. I bought a double driving game, and one called 'The House of the Dead' where you had to stand and shoot a gun at the screen. The third was a fruit machine. It was all the stuff that required co-ordination.

'Are you mad, Kay?' said my friend. 'He can't even walk. You have to be realistic.'

That made me angrier than ever. And, do you know what? Anger makes you even more determined. It's motivating, and I knew that I could help Stan get better and achieve his potential – no matter what that might mean.

Friends proved to be funny things. I have met wonderful people due to this tragedy. They have been my mainstay and have supported us both through thick and thin whether that was fundraising or just being there for a chat. Then, there were the other kind. Two *good* friends – or so I thought – suddenly stopped phoning or asking after us and no longer invited me to anything. It was as if they thought, *Well, we can't ask Kay now because she's on her own.* Because of what happened, my status had changed too. That was very hard to take. It was as if we'd both become invisible. We don't need friends like that – no one does. My husband, though changed, was very much alive and a huge part of my life.

And, love is infinitely stronger than any friendship.

In my spare moments, I would write thing down. Whether it was what had happened during the day or sometimes a bit of poetry. It was my comfort, my outlet, and someone to talk to when no one else was listening.

I don't want to give the impression that this was all about Stan. I was part of this equation too.

A brain injury to someone you love leaves you alone and confused – not to mention depressed. You examine what has happened over again, re-living the scenario of the days before, the event itself and the aftermath. Mostly people avoid you because they don't know what to say or how to react – perhaps afraid they may upset you further. That isn't possible. Like bereavement, it's isolating because nobody can help, no one can give you the hope you desperately need to cling to.

He's changed and so are you, probably forever.

Despite all the wishing, begging and pleading, nothing in the world is going to change what happened. There comes a moment when you realise that. It's the moment when shock, worry, grief and hopelessness all come together. It's the lowest moment anyone can sink emotionally.

But it *is* about you too. That is not selfish, but a fact. I had to come to terms with the new me and what that would mean. All my dreams for us as a couple, all my hopes and expectations of the life we'd lead growing old together had been dashed.

It was all a huge re-evaluation for me too, and it did not come easily.

But, eventually it *did* come – slowly, quietly.

You reach a point when you begin to divert your attention, not on the things he *can't* do, but the things he *can*. Any small improvement becomes a triumph, and with each small accomplishment you learn to love and appreciate yourself again. For it's you that have done that, have persevered when no one else had the time or the patience to try.

Stan had been provided with a basic wheelchair when he came home. It was *very* basic – and very heavy. My bad back meant that I couldn't push him around in it. We appealed to the RAF Benevolent fund of which Stan had been a member when he served. Along with the ACT Foundation, they provided us with an all-singing, all-dancing powered wheelchair. It went up and down, side-to-side, with various lifts here and there. It was a wonderful contraption that made a world of difference to both our lives. They also gave Stan an electronic tablet that he could learn to type words on. It held a memory bank of common phrases too and stored things he'd typed in previously. Even though Stan had been an IT technician, all that knowledge had been obliterated with the brain damage. The tablet took longer for him to learn. As usual, progress was very slow, but he got the hang of it eventually. Sometimes the words came out muddled, though we could usually work it out.

But it *was* communication. At last, my husband had the means to talk to me. We were unable to have a right good chin-wag, but it represented progress. He could tell me what he wanted, and I was grateful for that. I began to look forward to getting up each day for the new challenges it might bring and what, as a couple, we could achieve today – no matter how small. Little things become more precious and I was starting to love life again.

Even so, typing words slowly on a screen was a poor substitute for having a conversation. Though I would never forget what his voice sounded like – that lovely scouse accent – I longed to hear it spoken to me.

Just once more.

Two young physiotherapists came in a few days a week and they managed to get him to take a few steps with help. I cried and so did they. Stan had to re-learn everything. His memory bank had been wiped clean, experience of how to do things forgotten – restored to factory settings, so to speak. And just like a young child learning new skills, he too had to start the process over again, to re-establish those lost pathways in the brain that tell us how to do things.

His incontinence was a huge problem. He didn't know what signals to give me. I gave him a buzzer that he could squeeze, and slowly we began to understand each other. By the time he had been home for six weeks, bar a few mishaps, he was clean and dry – and the infection had disappeared. He was telling me what he needed without the use of words and I knew that if he could do this, he could do other things.

Initially, Stan was reluctant to leave the bed. He clearly felt safer there than in a chair and slept a great deal. Later down the line we gravitated back into the same bad – our own. It was lovely to sleep beside my husband again.

Then, came the bombshell that in the future one of his physiotherapists was being withdrawn. This was hopeless. Stan needed two people to stand him, to progress his walking and getting his legs to move. One was quite bent from the sheer length of time he'd spent immobile. I couldn't do it.

In utter desperation, I contacted my local MP again and explained our situation. She was truly wonderful. The next day, the second physiotherapist was re-instated.

Christmas 2008 came and went, but with the New Year, Stan was staying out of bed for longer.

He took to watching the television more – ice hockey which he'd never have dreamed of watching before and taking obvious delight when his beloved Liverpool were winning at football, sitting there with his supporter's scarf around his neck. I'd contacted the club after his injury and they'd given us a couple of posters to sell, the money from which I decided to spend on the games room. I had it painted in their colours and I was able to engage an artist to help.

Stan was unable to smile, unless you gave him a happy memory to do it to. But, I'll never forget the moment he was wheeled into that room and saw the Liverpool logo with all the colours. His face was a picture and his eyes said it all.

Presently, he was able to use the room. His ability to operate the games controls with his left hand was improving. His right hand was still bent inwards, the stroke-like effect since the operation. It gave him constant pain. I hoped he wasn't getting depressed, though how he managed not to, amazed me. If my life had changed to that extent, I'm sure I'd have just given up. I often wondered what he was really thinking. Perhaps in some strange way we don't understand, fear is taken away along with the devastation. I hope so. Then from some far horizon, came a tiny glimmer of light.

One of Stan's carers had just picked up a tiny puppy. 'Would Stan like to see it do you think, Kay?' she asked.

'Well, let's see,' I said. 'Go and get him.'

Moments later, she returned with a blanket and revealed a ball of fluff with big, round eyes peering out at the world. Gently, she placed the puppy on Stan's bed close to his hand. The two looked at each other for a moment before something wonderful happened. Stan's face broke into a huge smile as he reached out to stroke the little animal. The puppy nuzzled his hand and he was unable to take his eyes from it, the smile never leaving his face. It was the first time he'd smiled properly since the operation and I now knew what I had to do.

Something that proved to be the best therapy in the world!

'Stan, shall we get a dog?'

He nodded ferociously.

'What sort of a dog shall we get?'

There followed a long period of patient tapping on the tablet. He was clearly giving it a great deal of thought. Presently he handed me the tablet, smiling happily.

I burst out laughing. 'Stan, you must me joking – a standard poodle? They're enormous. I couldn't walk that with my back. Tell you what – we'll get a smaller poodle and pretend it shrunk in the wash.'

His eyes twinkled, and he nodded. The deal was sealed.

Heidi arrived in February and it was love at first sight. From the first moment, she and Stan were inseparable. His life had found new meaning. They instantly seemed to understand each other. Stan's gentle hand on her head soothed her and she'd gaze up at him, this ball of black fluff. There was a permanent smile on his face whenever he was near her and she seemed to know instinctively what he needed from her. Well, that was just the beginning. Hot on her heels in July came Chico – a black and tan dachshund, the typical sausage dog. Then a month later, Lily joined the clan, our black dachshund! We suddenly had become a much larger family.

Lily, Heidi and Chico

The Kids!

A Couple of Swells

It was becoming obvious that Stan's right hand was never going to recover its movement and seemed to be contracting inwards more and more. It was very painful and got in the way. The decision to have it removed was a momentous one, as it would require another anaesthetic and I was unable get it out it out of my mind what had happened last time. It was a balancing act between risks, but he needed to be pain-free to concentrate on other things.

We saw a hand surgeon who was able to confirm that it wasn't ever going to bc any use and with his professional manner managed to put both our minds at rest. We *did* use the NHS this time however and at the end of 2009, Stan's right hand was amputated just above the wrist. I hardly dare breathe until the moment he woke up and smiled at me.

Because of Stan's brain damage, he didn't suffer any sensations from the phantom limb syndrome that some amputees do. His recovery was uneventful, and he adapted to life without the inconvenience of a useless hand, getting in the way. Apart from a sniff or two, the dogs seemed unimpressed – provided they still got stroked and petted.

Handsome boy with a beard sporting his invincible look

*****

During the long nights when I couldn't sleep, I'd go over in my mind what we would do with any compensation we received – what new treatments and innovations would be open to us if, when it was all settled, we got a sizeable sum. But there *was* no compensation. Stan had been a private patient for his surgery and that makes a huge difference. There was no way of proving what had happened to Stan during that anaesthetic and surgery on his hip and no one was deemed to be responsible. No one would admit liability, and in the absence of hard evidence, we'd been told again by the Solicitor that culpability would be virtually impossible to prove.

That was awful. I didn't want to point the finger of blame at anyone in particular. What I desperately needed was a reason why my husband had sustained the irreversible brain damage that had destroyed both our lives. The lack of closure was like another insult piled on top of all the rest.

I'd heard about a wonderful new discovery that seemed to have endless possibilities. It involved stem cells. These are cells that are capable of producing others that can grow into any other type of cell in the body to repair damaged or worn-out ones. Apparently, mothers of newly-born infants were donating part of the umbilical cord – which is usually discarded shortly after birth – for research. Stem cells are abundant in the cord and can be harvested easily. I'd read that the Anthony Nolan Trust had a sort of bank facility for the storage of umbilical cords.

With new hope in my heart, I began to research everything I could lay my hands on about stem cell research and treatment. Stan had no feeling in his tongue and *that* I reasoned, was why he was unable to speak or eat. If by some miracle that feeling could be restored – and this new therapy did seem like a miracle break-through – then maybe it would help us restore Stan's lost sensations and perhaps he may be able to do those things again.

There were trials being done in Scotland but when I enquired, I was told that Stan didn't qualify as you had to be at least sixty-five. I found that incomprehensible! Any resulting treatment could only be done in America and China. No one else was offering it at that time.

So, it was back to the phones. The Americans were rather blasé about it all. They said to get over there and they would do it. I needed to ask very many more questions than they were prepared to answer, most of all, the success rate, how it was to be done, how it would affect Stan and most of all, what the cost would be.

The Chinese were much more helpful. No matter what silly questions I asked them, they answered simply and with patience. If we chose to go to China, they needed Stan's case-notes, scans and X-rays to be sent a couple of weeks before we arrived. The Americans asked for none of that. It was 'just get here and then we'll sort everything out.' I didn't feel that was good enough. There was no definition on the final cost either.

The Chinese told us exactly what was involved. All in as a package including flights, treatment and accommodation, it was £35.000! My heart sank. We hadn't the disposable funds for anything like that and with no forthcoming compensation, it all suddenly seemed futile. It was like a kick in the teeth, a pain in your soul and a feeling of sudden impotence – that you've gone as far as you can. All my senses said 'Fight, Kay.'

But, how could I? Where was I going to get that sort of money? It seemed that all my wishing, hoping and hours spent on research had been in vain.

However, fate hadn't finished with us yet.

A long-standing friend of Stan's got in touch. Mike Bates had served with him in the RAF, and he'd heard what happened to Stan. Now living in Saudi Arabia, he threw us a lifeline. Mike belonged to the Royal Antediluvian Order of Buffalos. I'd never heard of them, but he explained that a bit like the Masons they were able to raise money for good causes. They were a large group of like-minded, successful businessmen who banded together to give something back.

So, from his home in Saudi, Mike began the process of fundraising and later, presented us with a magnificent £8.000. Now it was my turn. I knew that with resolve – and a little help from others perhaps, I could raise the rest of the money needed. So, I set to work with a large piece of paper, listing every possible way we might raise money. I began to contact people. Everyone we knew, including the local pub, did their bit. I sold my mother's jewellery which raised £2.000. It was a good start. I soon realised that we needed to organise events. That would bring in the most money.

I wrote to various celebrities and organised posters, amazed at how, when they heard Stan's story were willing to help us by just coming along to support us. It also gave Stan a great opportunity to meet some of his heroes. I hardly recognised myself, I was so driven, but when you're fighting the corner of someone you love you don't give much thought to yourself. I knew I must do it for Stan to give him every chance of a better life. Some people stuck with us throughout and some fell away, but I was grateful for every penny that got us nearer to China.

A Voice For Stan

Exclusive Ball & Charity Auction
Hosted by James Lewis from bbc2 tv

Saturday 16th February

The Red Lion Bar & Bistro
Stone Edge, Chesterfield

Live band & 3 course meal included
£37 per ticket
Contact Kay on 01246 221932 / 07834 601008

The lovely James Lewis – Auctioneer supporting us at one of our fundraising events

A little bird told me

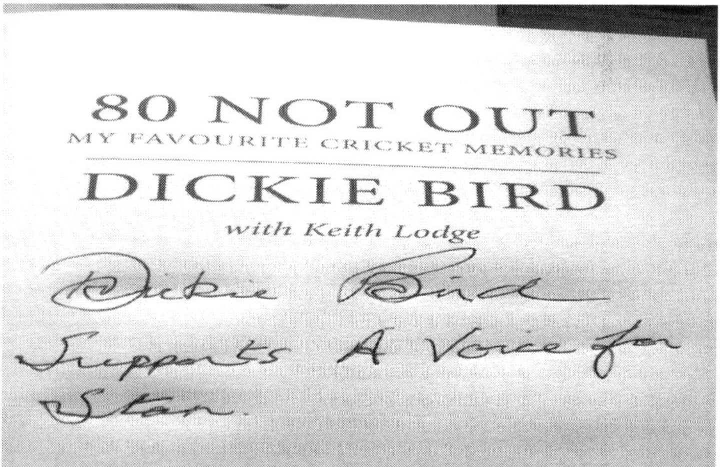

Dickie Bird – a lovely man and long-time cricket umpire

www.avoiceforstan.org
A Voice for Stan
Presents
Psychic Evening
WITH
psychic medium
steve rhino
Thursday 11th December
@ The Red Lion, Church Street
Brimington, Chesterfield
S43 1JG
7 pm
TICKETS £7 IN ADVANCE FROM KAY
01246 221932 07834601008
ALL TICKET SALES ARE GOING TO STAN'S APPEAL

Rotary Club Presentation.
They fundraised for us

This is Vanessa, our Osteopath, who worked voluntarily at the Rotary Club

Stan with Paul Martin - Host of the BBC's 'Flog It'

A momentous meeting with the inspirational Ben Parkinson who has also triumphed over adversity. They had an instant rapport

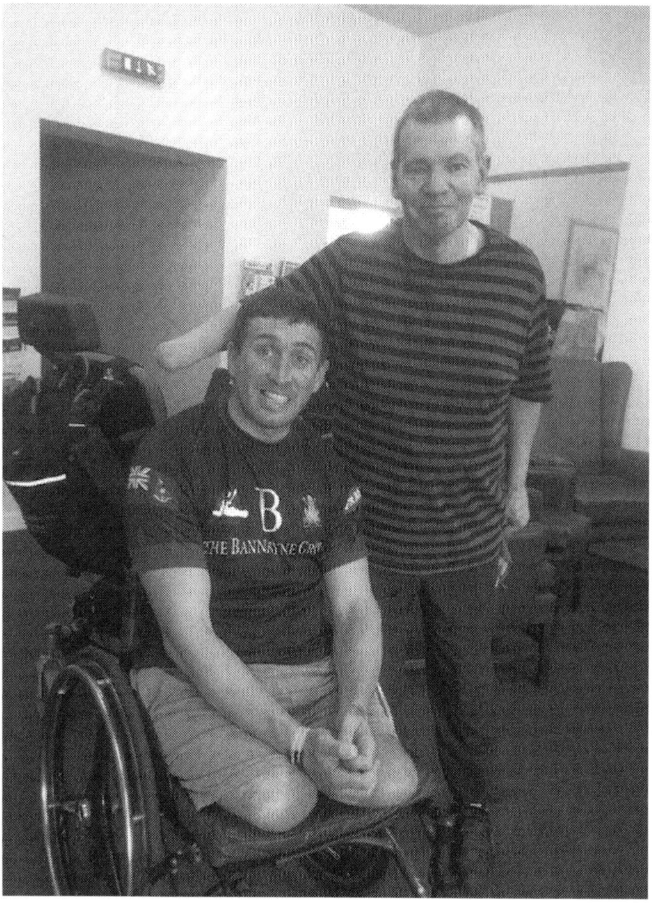

My cousin, Diane Harrison who helped us so much, raising over £8.000, and sadly lost her fight against cancer in 2015

Parkside Fitness Centre in Matlock

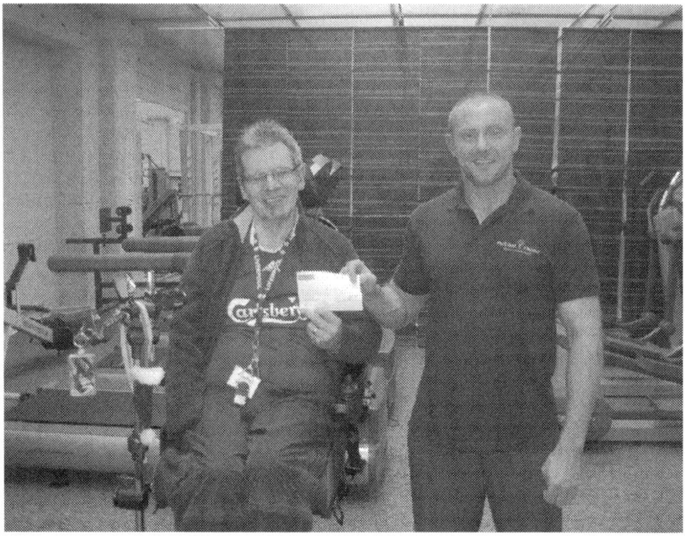

Another very welcome donation. People were so generous.

There were many more people who helped us raise the money that took us to our goal, and together we had done it. Finally, I began to believe that this was now a reality. We could go to China to give Stan the chance of a better life and one he so richly deserved.

I planned the trip with hope in my heart. I knew though, that not being the fittest person in the world myself, I couldn't make a long trip like that alone. It seemed that all our long-standing friends had work commitments and were unable to take the required four weeks off. So, I asked Jean, who I hadn't known for very long. She was retired. Initially reluctant, she eventually agreed.

Before the trip, all Stan's records, MRI scans, X-rays etc were sent over to China. There was also all his giving sets and bags of food that had to go a week before, as Stan is fed artificially straight into his stomach. Before we left, I rang the hospital and relaxed somewhat when I knew they had arrived.

The prospect of travelling such a large distance to China with a profoundly disabled man was daunting to say the least, and the lead up to it was stressful. Diane passed away two weeks before we left.

The journey out there went rather well. The airline was geared up to the process of loading him first and getting him settled before other passengers boarded, was efficient. We were met at Gatwick and Stan was transferred by staff from his electric wheelchair to a manual one. His own was then tagged and loaded onto the aircraft. A staff member was always on hand for us and pushed Stan through security, customs and passport control. It went very well. But we *were* travelling business class as we needed so much more room in the aircraft due to one of Stan's legs being permanently bent. Poor old Jean had to travel economy class to save money, but she didn't complain.

I was a bit concerned how a nine-hour flight would go as I've had two previous blood clots, but at least I could get up and move around. But the weeks leading up to going to China had been stressful, not least packing for a month away, when we didn't know what we'd need. It wasn't like going on holiday where you can make do if you've forgotten anything.

Packing for a trip of this length, apart from all the stuff Stan needed for his essential care was difficult. Although I'd looked online at the expected temperatures, a lot of the time we'd be inside. The question of how much stuff we'd need had to be considered within the weight limit. It wasn't exactly your two-week package holiday where if you were short of underwear, you could nip to the local market.

So, it was a case of taking a bit of everything.

The flight went well. Stan slept for quite a lot of it. We always joked he could sleep on a washing line, but I found it a bit gruelling – more like two days than nine hours, always aware that I must keep getting up and walking around. The last thing I needed was another blood clot. Because of the distance we lost a whole day. My body clock was confused to say the least.

We'd booked an apartment for the duration of our stay, so we could be near Stan throughout the treatment and had to employ a caregiver in China. They charged the princely sum of £20 per day – unbelievable when you look at the cost of care here. Jean would be staying at the apartment mostly, though there would be a bed provided in Stan's room. I decided that I would stay with him in his room on *the days he had his stem-cell therapy.*

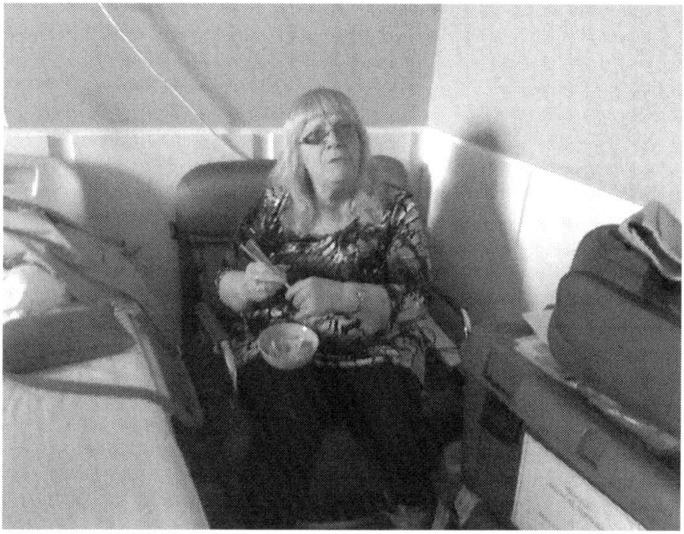

Jean practising 'Chopsticks"

Stan on the aircraft looking very smug. No wonder –
He'd slept for a good part of the flight.
And Liverpool went with him around his neck

Beijing – It was huge!

Pretty overwhelming after Chesterfield

The traffic had to be seen to be believed. How did anyone ever get anywhere?

We landed in Beijing and were met by helpers and taken to a rickety old ambulance/ bus for the trip to the hospital. It was an hour's bumpy ride through unimaginable traffic. I doubt they'd heard of suspension!

The hospital was palatial but there was building work going on with temporary buildings everywhere that could only be accessed by going outside. And, there was the health and safety – Oh my God. It was non-existent! An extension into an extension into a couple more extensions. It was anybody's guess what would have happened if it rained. Thank goodness it didn't. All the little Chinese men would have probably been sprinting around collecting all the plugs and cables before there was a bang and a flash, closely followed by the disappearance of the hospital.

Glad to be in China at last with one of the team

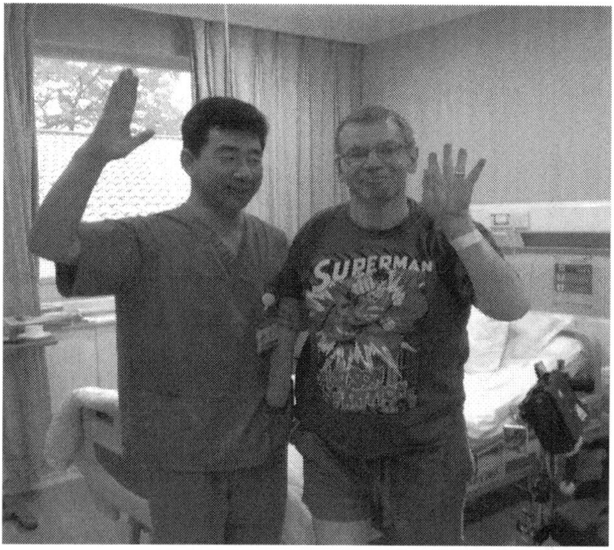

A little flash of bare leg there, Stan

Stan had a lovely room with an extra fold-away bed in it, and with an adjoining wet room.

The Chinese were so welcoming and made us feel very special. One or two of the doctors spoke a little English and we spoke no Chinese, but somehow, we all managed to get through with hand signals and some excellent method acting worthy of an Oscar.

We had the services of an interpreter, Aimi, who was excellent, though she wasn't there all the time. If we needed help though, reception would phone her immediately. And there was our appointed carer – a tiny Chinese woman who spoke not one word of English but kept turning up and cooking us dumplings. They were lovely. Jean and I nodded furiously making the expected appreciative noises of thanks. And then more dumplings arrived... and more... and more until I couldn't face another. But rather than insult her, we hid them in the most extraordinary places. Most found their way down the loo, so if the Beijing sewers overflowed, it would be all the dumplings that had finally backed up the system. We were able to cook in Stan's room. There was a small fridge and hob and we bought a steamer, so I could have fresh vegetables on the days I stayed. Can you imagine that happening in our hospitals? For a start, the smoke alarms would have gone off with the first whiff of steam, closely followed by Matron, who would most probably have ejected the lot of us into the street.

The Chinese certainly did things differently.

Stan was to have four stem-cell treatments in all, as well as acupuncture and a great deal of intensive physiotherapy. Stem-cell treatment nowadays is preceded by chemotherapy to knock out the immune system, but in China, it wasn't done like that. There was a therapist who worked on his tongue, attaching suction pads to pull it forward and stimulate it. It was certainly interesting to watch – if a bit alarming.

Stan went along with it all with his usual patience and fortitude.

The Tongue Dynasty Therapist

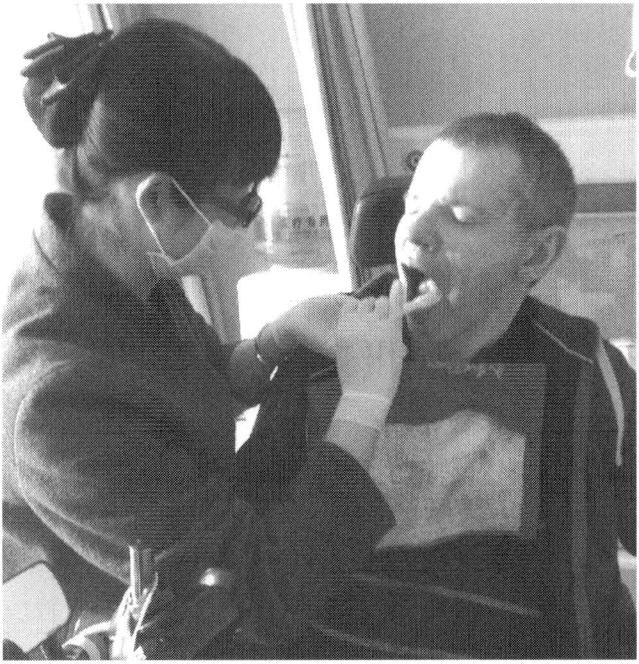

Acupuncture is a normal part of treatment in the east – for just about every ailment. In China, acupuncture has been practised since before recorded times, it is thought for at least 10,000 years. Needles were once made from stone and were called Bian Stone, meaning a sharp, narrow stone used for healing. Many have been found in ancient Chinese ruins, along with hieroglyphs showing the practice. The Chinese have remained proud of their art, though during the early 20th century, it fell from favour due to the spread of Western medicine. But it is very much back in fashion – worldwide – and is as relevant today as it was thousands of years ago.

It is linked to the belief that disease is caused by disruptions to the flow of energy within the body, or 'qi.' Basically, you put the needle through specific points in the body and stimulate the nerves.

One of the acupuncture sessions

To refresh the parts others can't reach –

Or

Stan's audition for the latest Pinhead film

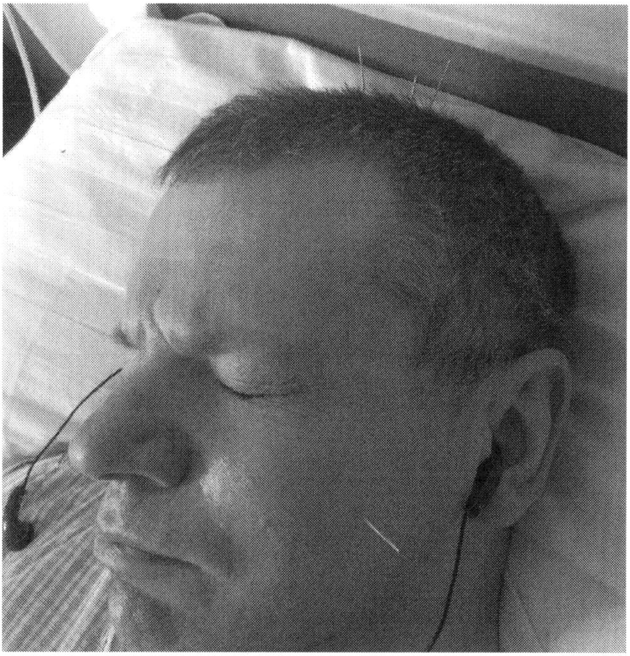

No slacking... This woman is a slave-driver, Kay

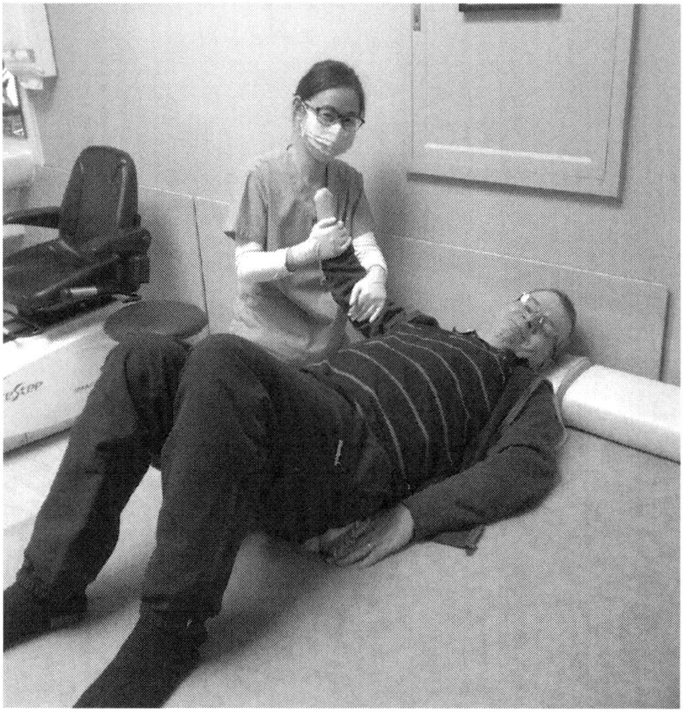

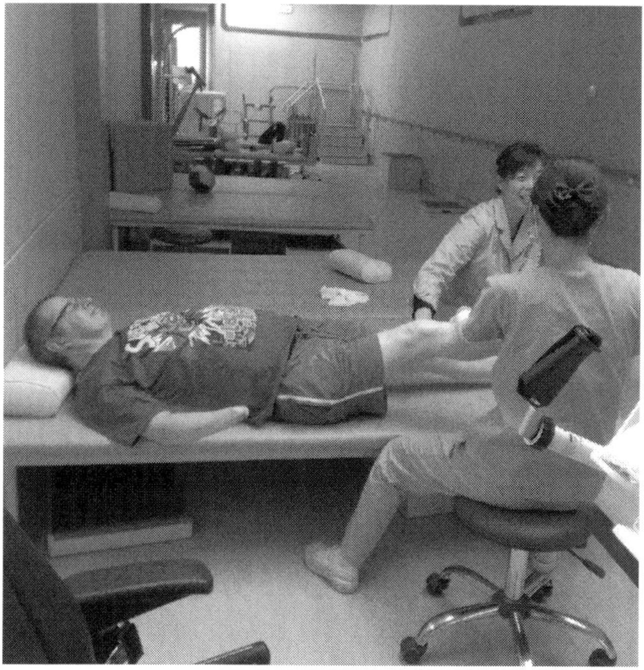

Next year it'll be the Beijing Marathon at this rate

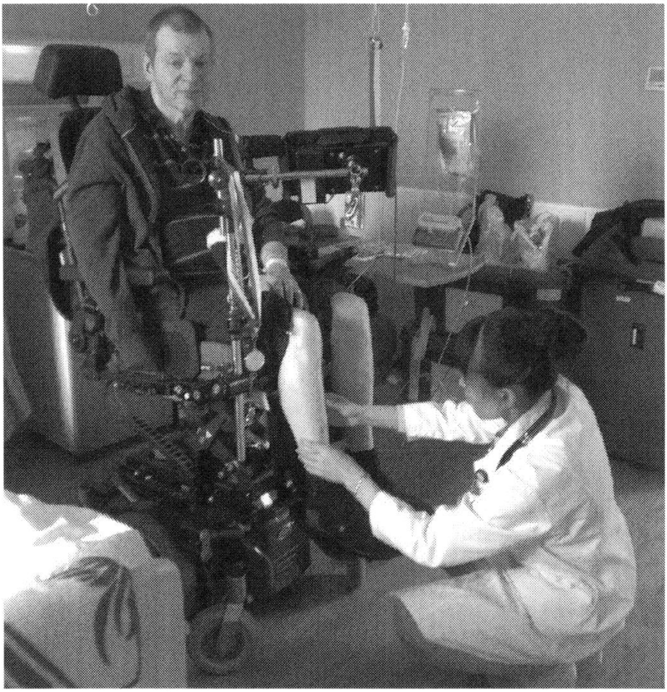

The wonderful Chinese Medical team.
Always smiling, happy and with endless patience

I stayed with Stan in his room each time he has his stem-cell treatment. I just needed to be near him. Jean was happy to stay at our rented apartment.

Before his first treatment, Stan had an MRI scan of his brain. His doctor who was doing the treatment not only came to collect him from his room but pushed him all the way to the theatre and back. Can you imagine that happening here? It was clearly all-hands-on-deck no matter how important you were. I waited while Stan was taken down to theatre where he was given a lumbar puncture. The stem-cells were then injected into his spine. It all took about half an hour and then he was returned to his room where he had to lay flat on his back for 6 hours before doing a gradual sit up. He was warned he may experience a headache after the treatment and did have one the next day.

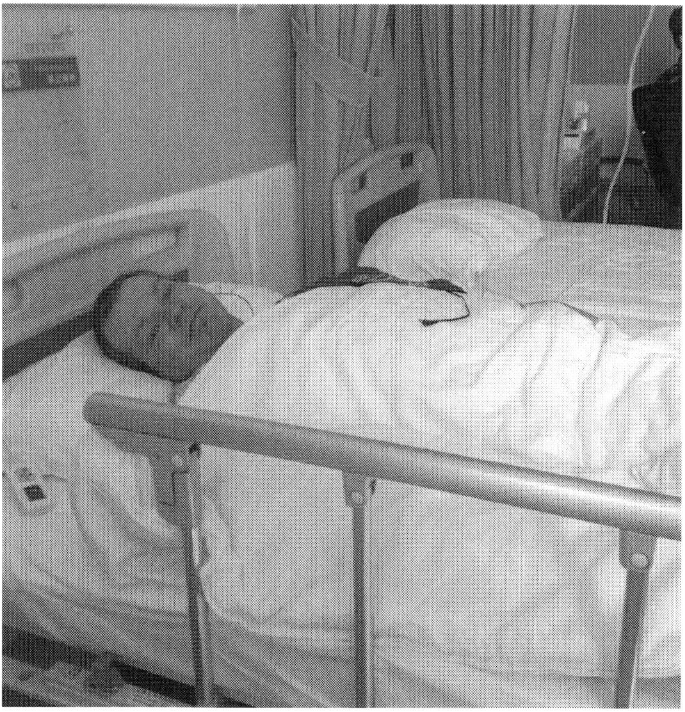

Flat out after treatment and a teensy bit impatient

Sitting in the hospital café one day, I met a lady from Texas called Dana. She was there with her son Joey and his wife. We began to chat as we were clearly the only Westerners in the place. Joey suffered from a condition he'd had from birth, some sort of rare dystrophy. He was unable to walk and had profound muscle weakness. 'Why didn't you have the treatment back home in America?' I asked Dana. She told me they had, but it hadn't worked, and this was their second trip to China. The first time, he'd had a great deal of improvement in his strength. Stan and he would visit each other quite often during our final week there. We remained in touch after we all returned home.

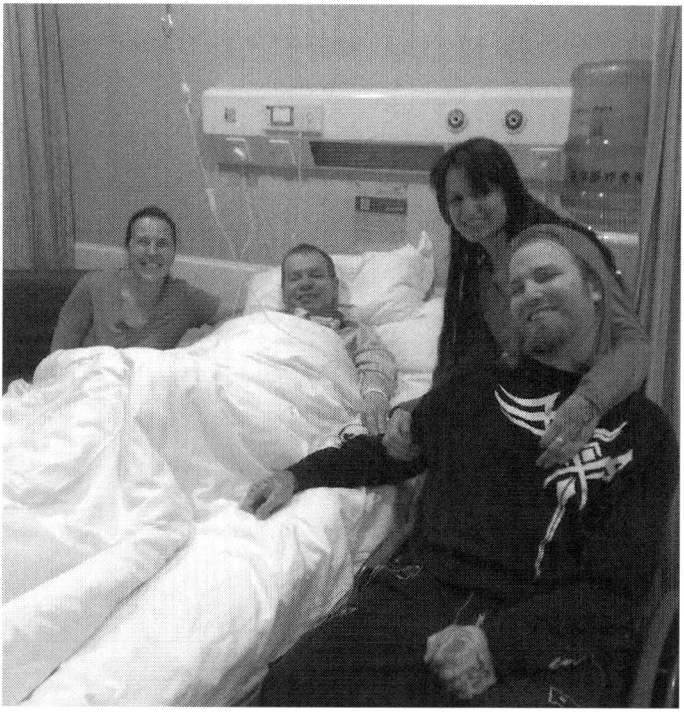

New friends from Texas

Joey and his family

Four weeks in a hospital room is a very long time and I asked the doctors if we could take Stan out in his wheelchair. No one had any objections provided we didn't want to go on the days when his stem-cell treatments were due with their scans and lumbar punctures.

That was wonderful, and we managed to see a few of the sights in Beijing. Once outside the private hospital though, it was a different world. People lived in little more than shacks with just a curtain for a door. It opened our eyes and made us feel sad to see how the ordinary people lived – the haves and the have-nots.

This was further underlined when one morning I woke up with such swollen eyes, I could have auditioned for a horror film. I was told I must go to the local hospital and the interpreter made me an appointment. She had warned me that the hospital I was going to, though only a ten-minute walk away, was nothing like the one we were in. I didn't really care at this point as I peered out from beneath grossly swollen eyelids. How bad could it be?

It was a very hot day. I walked into something that reminded me of pictures of a battlefield dressing-station during the war. There were stretchers lined up row on row, with sick people crammed in every corner. I almost had to fight my way through to Reception where I registered and for £5 was told that I could return there for life if I needed to! Within forty minutes, I'd seen an eye specialist, been given drops and was out of the place. Total cost, £10. The treatment worked quickly – much to my relief and we were able to go sightseeing with Jean. She'd done a lot of waiting about and it was good to give her a treat or two for her kindness in coming with us in the first place.

We visited The Temple of Heaven, that had been built in the Ming Dynasty around the same time as the Forbidden City. The Temple has magnificent architecture and is so colourful. I was so glad we had the time to visit it as no one should go to Beijing and not see it. The Hall of Prayer looks the same from every direction and feels like an optical illusion. It was built that way on purpose. The Jiajing Emperor had no son and he ordered this to demonstrate that his succession was by the will of heaven. He built it round instead of square as denotes yin and yang philosophy.

The beautiful Temple of Heaven,

Beijing

The Forbidden City, Beijing

Stan looks as though he's about to join the escape committee – though China is not wheelchair-friendly. Poor Jean had to do most of the man-handling up the pavements

Masked and wrapped in the Liverpool colours.
No one goes out without a mask as air pollution is a real problem

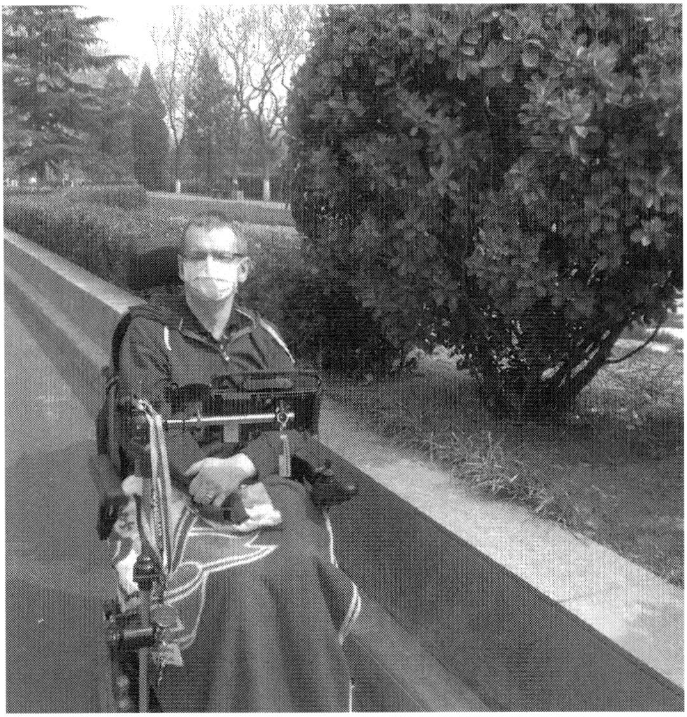

After the first stem-cell treatment, it was noticeable that Stan had started to get stronger. Initially, I thought it must be coincidence, but he felt better and most of all, he'd begun to get some sensation back in his tongue. It was very encouraging.

That sensation remains and is permanent. I hoped that if he got that back, his speech and ability to eat would follow in some way, but the problem was that there was underlying brain damage that couldn't be overcome. The link between his brain and tongue was severed and could not be reconnected. I knew then that I would have to be Stan's voice forever.

When we returned from China, it was clear that in other ways there had been a great improvement in the things Stan could do. He no longer fell asleep throughout the day and was much more alert. Before, he was unable to read more than a few words before he became exhausted. Suddenly, he could tackle the newspaper! He had renewed strength and actually started going to a gym and he could remember how to do things on his computer that he couldn't before.

An enormous step forward

With this renewed energy, Stan was able to be taken places, as he was much more alert – and he developed a love of ice-hockey which he'd never have dreamed of watching before. Sheffield Ice are geared up for the disabled and it allowed him to be taken to games. He'd go in style, in the full regalia.

At the Sheffield Steelers Ice Hockey game.

Please note the presence of his mascot Chloe who goes everywhere

Stan has a personal assistant and carers who have always been willing to take him out. That is great as I am not up to taking him as far as Sheffield. We once went on a trip to Lincoln for the day and I found it a challenge because of my back.

Along the way, we have met some wonderful people, and one of the best is Sam. We call her our adopted daughter who we've known now for four years. She is the loveliest, sweet-natured and pain-in-the-backside at times, girl you could ever have the pleasure of knowing. She has truly been my rock, unwavering in her support to us. We speak every day, either on her way to work or the way home. My only wish is that she could have known Stan as he was before. She does so much for us – always there, always willing to do things.

Me and my girl, Sam

Stan goes to bowls every week and used to walk up and down when playing. Unfortunately, he has developed arthritis in his other hip and now goes in his wheelchair with the carer by his side to pick up the bowls for him.

Like me, Stan is a Capricorn – he meets things head-on – sometimes thinking he can do things he can't, and he is prone to falls. A bit stubborn like most men!

I've always tried to keep everything as normal as possible – normal that is for us. It would get very boring for me and him if we just sat around the house all day watching television. But it is a major logistical operation to take Stan out. We plan meticulously for appropriate toilet stops with access where we can park the people-carrier he travels in with its lift on the back which requires space to load and unload. We've learned over the years, venues where the disabled are catered for well and which ones just do the basics that the law requires – and some not even that, despite legislation.

Stan's feeding tube needs to be flushed with water every two hours to keep him hydrated. Everything we need must be taken with us and be kept meticulously clean. Each day, he has an infusion of a bag of feed that is given slowly over 3-4 hours direct into his stomach. So, we have to know where we'll be and when and have to ensure we're not delayed.

But we have a life. We are still together and, despite everything the world has thrown at us, we are still very much in love. I said that when I took those marriage vows, it was forever and without proviso.

I fervently hope we will grow old together, Stan and me. It won't be the sort of life we planned or expected all those years ago, but it's ours because we have each other and that is the most important thing. After Stan's operation, I made a promise – that I would fight to make my husband's life as good as it could be, by giving him the voice that he had lost. I *became* his voice and I kept that promise.

A voice for Stan.

April 2018,

Twycross Zoo

Stan meets a new friend

A visit to the giraffes at Twycross Zoo

Feeding the giraffes with my son Matt

A beautiful day filled with happiness and memories

<u>I Wanna Grow Old with You : 'Westlife'</u>

Another day without your smile

Another day just passes by

But now I know how much it means

For you to stay right here with me

The time we spent apart will make our love go stronger

But it hurts so bad I can't take it any longer.

I want to grow old with you

I want to die lying in your arms

I want to grow old with you

I want to be looking into your eyes

I want to be there for you, sharing everything you do

I want to grow old with you

A thousand miles between us now

It causes me to wonder how

Our love tonight remains so strong

It makes our risk right all along

The time we spent apart will make our love grow stronger

But it hurts so bad I can't take it any longer

I want to grow old with you

I want to die lying in your arms

I want to grow old with you

This was our wedding song. It is very appropriate that it should appear here, now.

Author's Note

I first met Stan and Kay in the summer of 2017. I'd put up some posters in the local shops advertising my latest novel. Kay contacted me to ask if I ever did 'ghostwriting.' Although we lived only streets away, we'd never met, but I had heard of the 'A Voice for Stan' appeal. There was a large collecting jar on the bar of our local pub, the Barley Mow. The landlord was always very supportive of local good causes. Before then, I had been unaware of the circumstances, but a quick look on Facebook revealed the horrifying story. I've worked for the NHS in Chesterfield for 51 years as a nurse and midwife and it's true, we have one of the best healthcare systems in the world. However, I more than most, are acutely aware that occasionally things can go wrong – in Stan's case with devastating consequences.

I confessed I'd never ghost-written, but would Kay like me to pop over and see her?

Later that week, I met them – Stan, Kay and the dogs of course, who immediately tried to lick me to death. It was a meeting that would change my life.

They had little money and so I decided there and then that this was a story that was begging to be written. I'd do it for them for the love of doing so, because here were two wonderful people that had fought against almost impossible odds and had come out the other side – still together and still hopelessly in love. The one proviso I gave was that it would have to be done in my spare time and there wasn't much of that! I am still a working midwife, granny, writer and mummy to ten hives of bees. I estimated that it may take a year or more. They were very happy with that.

It became clear that Stan had been the most remarkable man who'd led a full and interesting life before the operation. He'd travelled the world with his work. And then there was Kay. She was something else. Married only two years before their lives changed forever, she'd ignored all those who'd told her that Stan must go into care. It wasn't out of duty because in her vocabulary, that word does *not* exist.

'When I took my wedding vows, I promised to love, honour and cherish him – in sickness and in health. No one mentioned an option to pick and choose. I love my husband, unconditionally and equally.

For all he was then and all that he is now.'

It was hard to control my emotions at the words of this special, attractive woman who had taken on what, for most of us would have been impossible. And she had succeeded. When the hospital had given him up as a profoundly disabled man with little quality of life, Kay had not.

It was she who fought like a tiger to get him to where he is today – a lovely guy who can engage in conversations electronically with people, who has no malice at his lot. He goes out on his 'wagon' scooting around the village on a nice day and has a fanatical love of sport – ice hockey and his beloved Liverpool football club, of course. And they have friends and carers willing to take him to events.

But money is short. Kay has been an inexhaustible fundraiser and craft worker, to bring in money to pay for the extras that enrich Stan's life. These are things not provided by the system. There may be money provided for basic care and strictly on a need basis, but isn't there more to life than that?

It's not just needs, but the whole body and mind is what we need to be looking at. I hope the politicians are listening!

We worked together on the book. I would visit to make notes and ask interminable questions and Kay would record all the rest on a cassette player. Stan is unable to be left for very long and so this worked well. We became good friends and sometimes it was easy to forget that Stan was disabled when I was there. We'd chat away and talk to Stan like anyone else and he'd tap away on his tablet.

Kay had suffered periods of ill-health throughout her adult life. She's not only had deep-vein thrombosis, but after her cousin Diane passed away from cancer, she discovered she also had the faulty gene BRACA 1. She opted for ovarian removal and a double mastectomy only a few months before they travelled to China.

In early March 2018, I gave Kay a lift to the doctor's surgery. She'd been having some 'tummy trouble'. They referred her to hospital and discovered a large malignant tumour in her bowel. It was inoperable as there were secondaries in her lungs, liver and lymph nodes. They gave her 6 months – a bit more if she had treatment with chemotherapy.

Stunned was an inadequate word.

Kay's wish was that the book was published before she passed and so everything took on a new urgency. If that's what Kay wished – then that's what she would have. Our grateful thanks must go to the wonderful Paul

Bohill of Channel 5's 'Can't pay? We'll take it away!' When he heard the story, he arranged publication of the book.

Kay has decided to have chemotherapy treatment to allow her to make plans for Stan's continuing care. She is still the same tour-de-force she always was, realising and accepting that by her death, Stan will be able to continue to live with care assistance in his own home – their home.

The terrible irony of this cannot escape any person who has the slightest empathy. Kay is philosophical about her diagnosis and is driven by completing what she wants to do – to see this book in print. I fervently hope that in some small way I have done a little towards that.

She is the bravest woman I know.

The final words in this book, must go to Stan. This is a text from him to me.

'I want you to know that Kay is my soul-mate and I love everything about her. I would not be where I am if it wasn't for her. I don't know how I will cope without her.'

Sue Pacey

May 17th 2018

Acknowledgements

Kay and Stan would like to express their special and heartfelt thanks to the following people.

Mike Bates – Royal Antediluvian Order of Buffalos

Neil Bennett – Chesterfield Charity Committee

Christopher Kay and Mark Cordingley

Debbie Beque-Bennett

Derby Gaol

Slimming World – Hasland

Parkside Fitness Centre – Matlock

Caz Stafford

Shamal Lodge – Saudi Arabia

The Barley Mow – Wingerworth

The Red Lion – Stonedge

Last Orders – Clay Cross

The ACT Foundation

Chester Street Club – Chesterfield

And many others who know who they are…

Available worldwide from

Amazon

---

www.mtp.agency

www.facebook.com/mtp.agency

@mtp_agency

All proceeds from the sale of this book will go towards the continuing care of Stan Martindale Padley

www.facebook.com/A-Voice-for-Stan-492674820767164/

27501265R00061

Printed in Poland
by Amazon Fulfillment
Poland Sp. z o.o., Wrocław